Where Plants and Animals Live

Vocabulary

- community
- desert
- ecosystem
- environment
- grassland
- population
- tundra
- wetland

WHAT ARE ECOSYSTEMS?

Places for Living Things

A living thing needs just the right environment. An environment is everything around a living thing. Plants and animals are living things. They need sunlight, water, and soil. They also need the right kind of weather. Sunshine warms the environment. It helps plants make their own food.

Climate is also important for an environment.
Climate is the weather a place has over many years.
Different environments have different climates.
Climate affects an environment's water and soil.
Water and soil affect the plants in an environment.
Plants need certain kinds of water and soil to live.

Parts of an Ecosystem

Plants and animals get what they need
from where they live. They interact with nonliving things in an ecosystem. The parts of an ecosystem work together. Redwood trees grow in a coastal ecosystem. Rain and fog from the ocean give them water. The parts of this ecosystem need each other. Some birds find fish to eat in the ocean. Then they fly to the redwood trees to make nests.

These trees are part of a coastal ecosystem.

Special Homes

Plants and animals both need a place to live. This place is their habitat. They get what they need from their habitat. Plants get light, air, water, pollinators, and space to grow. Animals get food, water, and a space to live and grow.

If a part of a habitat is missing, the plants and animals can't live there. They might not get what they need to live. They might have to move to a new place.

Dune grass grows in a habitat with sand.

Groups Within Ecosystems

Living things of one kind that live in the same place at the same time are a **population.** Southern California has many coyote populations. They live on brushy hillsides.

Squirrels live on the hillsides too. Coyotes hunt the squirrels. The coyotes, squirrels, and other living things in the ecosystem make up a **community.**

These two coyotes are part of a population.

Ecosystems Change

Sometimes ecosystems change. First, one part of the ecosystem changes. This causes other parts to change.

If it rains a lot in Southern California, plants will grow more. Squirrels have more food to eat. The squirrel population increases. More squirrels mean more food for coyotes. The coyote population increases too.

Squirrels and coyotes are part of the community in this hillside ecosystem.

What are ecosystems?

Places for Living Things

A living thing needs just the right environment. An **environment** is everything around a living thing. Plants and animals are living things. They need sunlight, water, and soil. They also need the right kind of weather. Sunshine warms the environment. It helps plants make their own food.

Grassland plants have long roots. They can get water that soaks deep into the soil. Winter frost kills plant leaves. Roots store food to grow new leaves in spring. Grazing and fire kill leaves too. New leaves grow from the roots.

Some grasslands get more rain than others. Tall grasses grow there. Short grasses grow where there is less rainfall.

How much rain do you think this grassland gets?

Desert—A Surprising Ecosystem

A **desert** is a place that gets little rain. During the day, it is usually very hot. At night it is cool or even cold. Plants and animals that don't need much rain live there. Cactus plants can live in the desert. They store water in their stems.

This desert is very dry.

Many desert animals hide during the hot day. Some stay in tunnels under the ground. Others rest under plants. Desert animals go looking for food at night, when it's cool. Snakes find and eat small animals. Bobcats hunt for birds and small animals to eat.

Sidewinder rattlesnake

Desert bobcat

Tundra—Land of Long Winters

The **tundra** is a place that is very cold and dry. It is near the North Pole. Tundra winters are long and cold. Tundra summers are short and cool. Tundra soil stays frozen underground all year.

Summer days in the tundra are very long. The Sun shines twenty-four hours a day on some parts of the tundra during summer. Winter days in the tundra are very short. In some places, the Sun doesn't shine at all in the winter.

A group of wolves is called a pack. Wolves hunt in the tundra in packs.

A group of caribou is called a herd. The herd stays together in the tundra.

Trees can't grow in the tundra. Their roots can't
grow in the frozen soil. Small plants, such as grasses
and wildflowers, can grow there.
The snow melts during the tundra summer. It
forms ponds. Birds make nests near the ponds. In the
summer they find insects to eat. Most tundra birds fly
to warmer places in the winter.

Why can't trees grow
in the tundra?

What are some forest ecosystems?

Coniferous and Deciduous Forests

Coniferous forests grow where the winters are cold and snowy. Coniferous trees have leaves like needles. Spruce and pine trees are coniferous trees.

Most plants can't grow under conifer trees. Some animals can live under conifer trees. They can find food and shelter in the coniferous forest.

North American coniferous forest

Deciduous forests grow where there are rainy summers and snowy winters. Oak and maple trees are deciduous. Deciduous trees drop their leaves in the fall.

More sunlight reaches down through deciduous forests. That allows plants to grow. Many animals can live in a deciduous forest. Insects and birds live in the plants and trees.

North American deciduous forest

Tropical Forests

Tropical forests grow where it is warm all the time. These forests get lots of rain. Many tall trees grow in tropical forests. Little sunlight reaches the gound in tropical forests. Many plants grow on the tall trees so they can get sunlight. Most of the animals live in the trees too.

Birds and insects live in tropical forests. There are many different tropical forest insects. There are so many that we haven't named them all!

Tropical forests are full of amazing animals. One tropical forest in Brazil has beetles that don't live anywhere else. Some tropical forest spiders are big enough to eat birds!

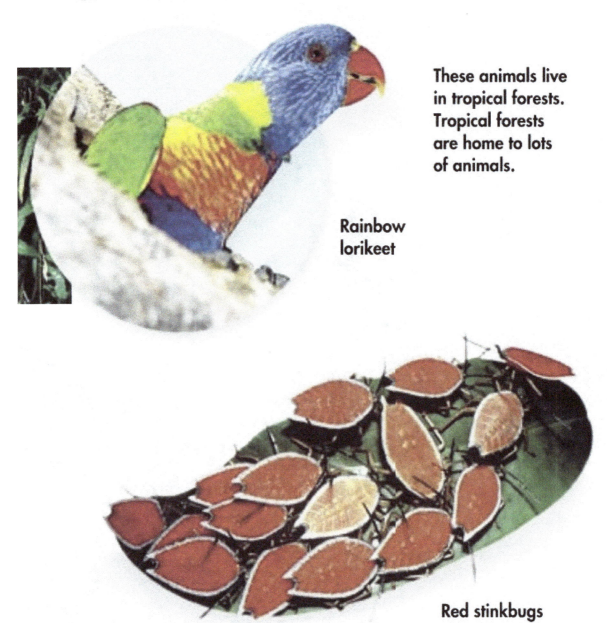

These animals live in tropical forests. Tropical forests are home to lots of animals.

Rainbow lorikeet

Red stinkbugs

What are water ecosystems?

Freshwater Ecosystems

Places that have fresh water include lakes, ponds, rivers, and streams. Lakes and ponds have land all around them. In rivers and streams the water moves.

Some of these places get fresh water from under the ground. Other places get water from rain or snow. Many plants and animals live in places with fresh water.

A **wetland** is low land that is covered with water. The water is there most of the year. But it is not very deep. Trees, grasses, and plants live in a wetland. Some of the animals that live there are fish, bears, and birds.

Alligator

Manatee

These animals live in wetlands. Manatees eat the plants that grow there. Alligators eat the fish and birds that live there.

Saltwater Ecosystems

Oceans contain salt water. Oceans are shallow near the land. Clams, crabs, and fish all live near the shore.

The water gets deeper as you move away from land. Fish, shrimp, and whales live in deeper water. Water far below the surface is dark and cold. No plants and few animals can live there.

Do you think these animals are found in deep or shallow water?

Cuttlefish

Coral reef

Many rivers flow into the ocean. Fresh river water mixes with salty ocean water. When this happens, a salt marsh can form.

A salt marsh is a kind of wetland. Special plants and animals live in a salt marsh. They can live in water and soil that has salt. Many fish, crabs, and other animals are born in salt marshes.

Our Earth has many different ecosystems. Ecosystems are always changing. Ecosystems change when the climate changes. They change when animals move out of them or into them. They change in many ways.

Ecosystems give us and other living things everything needed to live! Without ecosystems, there could not be life.

Glossary

community   all of the different groups of living things found in one place

desert   a place that gets very little water

ecosystem   all of the living and nonliving things interacting in an environment

environment   everything surrounding a living thing

grassland   a place with lots of grasses and few trees

population   living things of the same kind living in one place

tundra   a flat, treeless place that is very cold and dry

wetland   a place that is covered in shallow water for most of the year

CPSIA information can be obtained
at www.ICGtesting.com
Printed in the USA
BVHW021444290123
657300BV00012B/501